PRAISE FOR SOME (
ROSEMARY ELLEN GUILEY'S
PREVIOUS INSPIRING WORKS

The Miracle of Prayer

"Prayer heals. . . . *The Miracle of Prayer* honors our rediscovery of this ancient realization. Anyone facing illness or other problems will be inspired by Rosemary Guiley's magnificent account. There's no hype in these pages, and Guiley isn't selling any particular religion. She honors the majesty, the power, and the mystery of prayer in an evenhanded, admirable way. This is a wonderful book, straight from the heart."

—Larry Dossey, M.D., author of
Healing Words and *Recovering the Soul*

Angels of Mercy

"So impressive I bought a half-dozen copies to give away to friends."

—Rev. Grace B. Bradley,
Sparrow Hawk Villager (OK)

Tales of Reincarnation

"Filled with information. . . . As an introduction and overview, this book is excellent."

—*FATE* magazine (St. Paul)

Books by Rosemary Ellen Guiley

The Miracle of Prayer
Blessings: Prayers for the Home and Family
Wellness: Prayers for Comfort and Healing
Angels of Mercy
Tales of Reincarnation

WELLNESS

Prayers for Comfort and Healing

COMPILED BY

Rosemary Ellen Guiley

POCKET BOOKS

New York   London   Toronto   Sydney   Tokyo   Singapore

POCKET BOOKS, a division of Simon & Schuster Inc.
1230 Avenue of the Americas, New York, NY 10020

ISBN: 0-671-53715-6

First Pocket Books hardcover printing February 1998

10   9   8   7   6   5   4   3   2   1

POCKET and colophon are registered trademarks of
Simon & Schuster Inc.

Cover illustrations by Lina Levy
Design by Stanley S. Drate/Folio Graphics Co. Inc.

Printed in the U.S.A.

Contents

VII

Preface

*B*y far the majority of the prayers that we humans direct to the Divine concern requests for healing. Most often we ask for healing of the body, but also we ask for healing of mind and spirit. Our need to be healed supercedes all desires save for love, and all other needs save for basic survival. So often in life, the heart aches with wounds that cannot be assuaged save for comfort from the Divine. There is no greater way to reach God than through prayer.

This collection of prayers from around the world is intended to help the healing of any challenging circumstances in life. There are prayers to help cope with losses, setbacks, difficult times, and spiritual suffering. There are prayers for healing and wellness. There are prayers to help the contemplation of leaving life in the body, as well as to help the grieving process in death and mourning.

While it is important in the healing process to acknowledge and honor our wounds, the healing process is not complete without a refocusing of our attention on spiritual upliftment. We must raise ourselves from the blackness of despair into the light of renewal. Healing cannot fully take place until we rise like the phoenix from the ashes of our sorrowing.

To this end, this collection also includes prayers for forgiveness and compassion; prayers for celebrating nature, the divine, and the mysterious origins of life; and prayers of exaltation and happiness.

True healing must come first at the soul level. Healing does not always mean cure. We heal through prayer, which aligns our souls with God. By aligning ourselves with the Mind of God—the highest possible state of unconditional love, joy, and wholeness—we can overcome anything, be healed of all afflictions.

—*Rosemary Ellen Guiley*

Annapolis, 1997

I

Prayers for
Healing
and *Well-Being*

For All Good Things

*L*oving God, who sees in us nothing that you have not given yourself, make my body healthy and agile, my mind sharp and clear, my heart joyful and contented, my soul faithful and loving. And surround me with the company of men and angels who share my devotion to you. Above all let me live in your presence, for with you all fear is banished, and there is only harmony and peace. Let every day combine the beauty of spring, the brightness of summer, the abundance of autumn, and the repose of winter. And at the end of my life on earth, grant that I may come to see and know you in the fullness of your glory.

(*St. Thomas Aquinas, 1225–74*)

Prayer for the Sick

I hurt again, Lord,
I hurt all over.
From the very onset of my sickness,
I rebelled against pain,
I hid behind my medicine bottles,
I threw myself at You
in what must have been pure melodrama,
begging a reprieve.
Yet somehow You must have seen
something valuable about pain
because it's still here.
I suppose I should be thankful,
but I'm not very heroic.
I can't smile with gratitude
when my body is on the torture rack.
All I ask, Lord,
is that You help me grasp
the worth of the hurt twisting inside me,
because if I knew that,
maybe I'd be able to bear up better,
maybe then I wouldn't be so cranky
with those I love most.
But no matter what, Lord,
just help me get through today
without being too much of a burden.

(Max Pauli, modern)

For Healing

*L*ord, bless all means that are used for my recovery, and restore me to my health in thy good time; but if otherwise thou hast appointed for me, thy blessed will be done. O draw me away from an affection for things below, and fill me with an ardent desire after heaven. Lord, fit me for thyself, and then call me to those joys unspeakable and full of glory, when thou pleasest, and that for the sake of thy only Son, Jesus, my Savior. Amen.

(Thomas Ken, 1637–1711)

Dear Great Physician

Dear Great Physician, we thank you for the gift of healing that lies within the body, for the person who has health, has hope, and the one who has hope has everything. Lord, teach us that true and total healing including healing of the soul, of attitudes, and of relationships.

Lord, we may be whole in body but sick in soul and spirit. Help us to ask for your touch of healing to establish a right relationship with you, for from that source other healings flow.

We ask this in your name.

Amen.

(Gerrit Schut, modern)

For Physicians and Nurses

Almighty God, who dost inspire the hearts of all who would serve thee, we beseech thee to give thine especial blessing unto all physicians and nurses who care for the sick and the afflicted. Give faithfulness and skill to their work, efficiency to the means that they employ, and make them to realize that in their best service, they are serving thee. In the name of the Divine Physician, Christ our Lord. Amen.

(Christian, date unknown)

On the Good Use of Sickness

Y ou gave me health that I might serve you; and so often I failed to use my good health in your service. Now you send me sickness in order to correct me. My health was full of pride and selfish ambition when I was healthy. Now please let sickness destroy that pride and ambition. Render me incapable of enjoying any worldly pleasures, that I may take delight in you alone. Grant that I may adore you in the lonely silence of my sick bed. And grant that, having ignored the things of the spirit when my body was vigorous, I may now enjoy spiritual sweetness while my body groans with pain.

(Blaise Pascal, 1623–62)

For One Who Is Ill

O Father of mercies and God of all comfort, our only help in time of need; we humbly beseech thee to behold, visit, and relieve thy sick servant for whom our prayers are desired. Look upon him in thy mercy; comfort him with a sense of thy goodness; and give him patience under his affliction. In thy good time, and using all wise means, restore him to health, and enable him to lead his life to thy glory; and grant that he may finally dwell with thee in life everlasting.

(Christian, date unknown)

For Those in Mental Darkness

O Heavenly Father, we beseech thee to have mercy upon all thy children who are living in mental darkness. Restore them to strength of mind and cheerfulness of spirit, and give them health and peace.

(Christian, date unknown)

Thanksgiving for Recovery

O Father of mercies, we thank thee in behalf of [name] whom thou hast restored to health. We cried unto thee, and thou hast healed him. We trusted in thee, and thou hast helped us. Therefore will we praise thy name together. Grant, O Lord, that the life which thou hast saved may be more entirely devoted to thy service, and that we may learn to love thee, and trust in thee more and more.

(Christian, date unknown)

For the Sick

O Christ our Lord, who art the Physician of salvation, grant unto all who are sick the aid of heavenly healing. Look upon all faithful people who are sick and who love to call upon thy name, and take their souls into thy keeping, and vouchsafe to deliver them from all sickness and infirmity.

(Christian, date unknown)

For a Sick Child

*M*ost merciful Savior, who lovest little children, and thyself didst live as a little child upon the earth, we come to thee in behalf of one whom we love. Thou art the Good Shepherd and carest for the lambs of thy flock, leading them tenderly and bearing them in thy gentle arms. Bring thou this child, for whom our prayer is offered, safely through the time of sickness and danger. Teach him to be meek and loving and obedient like thyself. Keep him from all fretfulness and impatience. Let him feel that thou art ever near. Let him learn to love thee better and better. And if thou art pleased to restore him to health, make him to walk all his days, be they many or few, in the way that leadeth to eternal life. Hear us, O pitiful and loving Lord, who, with the Father and the Holy Ghost, livest and reignest one God, world without end.

(Christian, date unknown)

Healing Prayer to Make a Person Whole

Happily I recover.
Happily my interior becomes cool.
Happily I go forth.
My interior feeling cool, may I walk.
No longer sore, may I walk.
As it used to be long ago, may I walk.
Happily, with abundant dark clouds, may I walk.
Happily, with abundant showers, may I walk.
Happily, with abundant plants, may I walk.
Happily, on a trail of pollen, may I walk.
Happily, may I walk.

(Navajo Night Chant, date unknown)

Heal My Heart

Ah, Lord God, Thou holy Lover of my soul, when Thou comest into my soul, all that is within me shall rejoice. Thou art my Glory and the exultation of my heart; Thou art my Hope and Refuge in the day of my trouble. Set me free from all evil passions, and heal my heart of all inordinate affections; that, being cured and thoroughly cleansed, may I be made fit to love, courageous to suffer, steady to persevere. Nothing is sweeter than Love, nothing more courageous, nothing fuller nor better in heaven and earth; because Love is born of God, and cannot rest but in God, above all created things. Let me love Thee more than myself, more love myself but for Thee; and in Thee all that truly love Thee, as the law of Love commandeth, shining out from Thyself.

(Thomas à Kempis, 1379–1471)

In the Hospital

*L*ord, I don't want always to be filled with self-pity. But I do need the divine comfort which comes only from you. Thank you for the love of my family and friends and their encouragement which means so much to me just now. Most of all, though, I am grateful for your divine and loving care during these days I am here in the hospital. I praise your name through Jesus Christ.

(Hoover Rupert, modern)

Praise for Recovery from Sickness

*H*eavenly Father, we thank Thee that Thou hast been mindful of our prayer, that Thou hast so graciously turned our sorrow into joy, and hast restored us to health.

Continue Thy mercy. May cheerfulness of spirit and vigor of mind, and strength of body be daily granted. May the lesson learned in the illness be remembered and any occasion for a new attack be warded off.

We bless Thy Holy Name for all Thy goodness, for all the way in which Thou dost lead and for all Thou are doing day by day.

May the remembrance of Thy great goodness make us humble, holy, obedient and full of praise.

We ask it all in the name of our Redeemer, who forgiveth all iniquities, healeth all our diseases, redeems our life from destruction and crowns us with loving kindness and tender mercies, and satisfieth our mouth with good things.

(Abbie C. Morrow, modern)

For the Sick

O Lord, look down from heaven, behold, visit, and relieve this thy servant. Look upon him with the eyes of thy mercy, give him comfort and sure confidence in thee, defend him from the danger of the enemy, and keep him in perpetual peace and safety.

(Christian, date unknown)

For Those in the Healing Arts

O merciful Father, who hast made man's body to be a temple of the Holy Ghost, sanctify, we pray thee, all those whom thou hast called to study and practice the arts of healing the sick, and the prevention of disease and pain. Strengthen them in body and soul, and bless their work, that they may themselves live as members and servants of Christ, and give comfort to those whom he lived and died to save.

(Christian, date unknown)

To Ease Suffering

Almighty Father, we commend to thy loving care all who suffer, especially the sick in body and mind. Grant them patience in their suffering; cheer and uphold them with the knowledge of thy love; and if it be thy will restore them to health and strength.

(Christian, date unknown)

A Prayer for Well-Being

Hearken, O Earthmaker, our father, I am about to offer tobacco to you. My ancestor concentrated his mind upon you, and that with which you blessed him I now ask of you directly. I ask for the small amount of life you granted him, and for four times the blessings you bestowed upon him. May I never meet with trouble in life.

O Grandfather, chief of the Thunderbirds, you who live in the west, here is a handful of tobacco. Extend to me the deer with which you blessed my ancestor. I pray to accept this tobacco from me. May I never meet with trouble in life.

O Grandfathers, spirits of the night, walkers in darkness, to you I offer tobacco and ask for the fireplaces which my ancestor received. If you smoke this tobacco see to it that I never become a weakling.

To you who live in the south, you who look like a man, you who are invulnerable, you who deal out life from one side of your body and death from the other, you whom we call Disease Giver, to you I offer tobacco. In daylight, in broad daylight, did you bless my ancestor. With food you blessed him; you told him that he would never fail in anything, you told him that you would avoid his home; you placed animals in front of him that he should have no trouble in obtaining them. An offering of tobacco I make to you that you may smoke it and that I may not be troubled in life.

(Winnebago, date unknown)

Tend Thy Sick Ones

*T*end thy sick ones, O Lord Christ; rest thy weary ones; bless thy dying ones; soothe thy suffering ones; shield thy joyous ones; and all for thy Love's sake.

(St. Augustine, 354–430)

For Serious Illness

Out of my depths I cry to you, Lord! I know you hear my voice, I need power beyond my own to cope with what faces me here. Help me to have faith enough to respond to your love and grace and to gain the strength I need to master this time of illness. In the name of your son, the great healer, Jesus Christ, I pray.

(Hoover Rupert, modern)

For Health and Strength

Almighty God, who art the only source of health and strength, the spirit of calm and the central peace of the universe, grant unto us, thy children, such a consciousness of thine indwelling presence as may give us utter confidence in thee. In all pain and weariness and anxiety may we throw ourselves upon thy fatherly care, that, knowing ourselves guarded by thy loving omnipotence, we may permit thee to give us health and strength and peace.

(Christian, date unknown)

For the Sick

*F*old in thy compassion, loving Jesus, those who are smitten with disease. Lay a healing hand upon the wounds of their souls, that inner peace may be their portion. Revive their failing strength and let life conquer death in their ailing bodies, that rejoicing in thy mercy they may serve thee with grateful hearts all their days upon earth.

(Christian, date unknown)

Refuge

O God, our Refuge in pain, our Strength in weakness, our Help in trouble, we come to Thee in our hour of need, beseeching Thee to have mercy upon this Thine afflicted servant. O loving Father, relieve his pain. Yet if he needs must suffer, strengthen him, that he may bear his sufferings with patience and as his day is, so may his strength be. Let not his heart be troubled, but shed down upon him the peace which passeth understanding. Though now for a season, if need be, he is in heaviness through his manifold trials, yet comfort him, O Lord, in all his sorrows, and let his mourning be turned into joy, and his sickness into health.

(Christian, date unknown)

For a Person About to Undergo an Operation

W̶e beseech Thee, Lord Jesus Christ, to fill the heart of thy servant with utter trust in thee, that he may have faith to say, "Though I am sometime afraid, yet put I my trust in Thee." May he feel underneath him the everlasting arms, and rest in them. By those wounds and bruises, which thou bearest for us, look graciously upon the suffering body of this thy servant, and bless the means employed for his cure, and grant that he may so patiently endure all his suffering that the wounding of his body may be to the salvation of his soul.

(Christian, date unknown)

Medicine Formula

(to be shouted to the new moon)

I shall prosper,
I shall yet remain alive.
Even if people do say of me,
"Would that he died!"
Just like thee shall I do,
Again shall I rise.
Even if all sorts of evil beings devour thee,
When frogs eat thee up,
Many evil beings—lizards,
even when those eat thee up,
Still dost thou rise again.
Just like you will I do in time to come.
Bo!

(Takelma, date unknown)

A Prayer During Illness

O God our heavenly Father, Who knowest our weakness and wilt not lay upon us more than we can bear, help us to bear it patiently. May we through suffering learn to love Thee better, for Jesus Christ's sake.

(Christian, date unknown)

For the Medical and Nursing Professions

O Lord Jesus Christ, Who alone hast power over life and death, over health and sickness, give power, wisdom and gentleness to all Thy ministering servants, our doctors and nurses, that always bearing Thy Presence with them, they may not only heal but bless, and shine as lamps of hope in the darkest hours of distress and fear, Who with the Father and the Holy Ghost livest and reignest ever one God, world without end.

(Society for the Propagation of the Gospel, 1701)

For Those Who Tend the Sick

O Almighty God, Who didst send Thy Blessed Son to be the Great Physician of souls and bodies, look, we beseech Thee, upon Thy servants, to whom Thou hast committed the care of the sick. Bless, Lord, the remedies which they employ, help them ever to remember that in ministering to others, they minister to Thee; give them grace to be tender and patient, in all their work and service, and being mindful of their own last hours may their hearts be filled with sympathy and love, for the sake of Christ Jesus our Lord.

(Rev. A. McCheane, nineteenth century)

Patience

There, the sun is about to rise
and the whisper of morning is waiting
Patience heals a hungry heart
like the sun brightens the darkness of night.

(Joann Marie Everett, modern)

II

Prayers for
Transition
from Life

My Last Song

*L*et all the strains of joy mingle in my last song—the joy that makes the earth flow over in the riotous excess of the grass, the joy that sets the twin brothers, life and death, dancing over the wide world, the joy that sweeps in with the tempest, shaking and waking all life with laughter, the joy that sits still with its tears on the open red lotus of pain, and the joy that throws everything it has upon the dust, and knows not a word.

(Rabindranath Tagore, 1861–1941)

Bring Me into Your Presence

I beseech you, good Jesus, that as you have graciously granted to me here on earth to enjoy the sweetness of your wisdom and truth, so at death you will bring me into your presence, that I may see the beauty of your face, and listen to your voice which is the source of all wisdom and truth.

(Bede, c. 673–735)

A Prayer for the Dying

Bind the sick man to Heaven, for from Earth he is being torn away!
Of the brave man who was so strong, his strength has departed.
Of the righteous servant, the force does not return,
In his bodily frame he lies dangerously ill.
But Ishtar, who in her dwelling, is grieved concerning him, descends from
    her mountain unvisited of men.
To the door of the sick man she comes.
The sick man listens!
Who is there? Who comes?
It is Ishtar, daughter of the Moon God!
Like pure silver may his garment be shining white!
Like brass may he be radiant!
To the Sun, greatest of the gods, may he ascend!
And may the Sun, greatest of the gods, receive his soul into his holy
    hands!

(Ancient Assyrian, date unknown)

Prayer for a Holy Death

O blessed Michael, on thy name I call,
And on thine, O John the Baptist,
On the saints of the world, one and all,
For help in the coming day of battle.

When my mouth is closing and my eye is failing,
And my sense from me is slipping away,
When my term is spent and my cause a-calling,
God with my soul that dreadful day. Amen.

(Gaelic, date unknown)

An Inca's Death Prayer

O Creator of men thy servant speaks.
Then look on him
The king of Cusco.
Do not forget me
O thou noble creator.
O thou of my dreams.
Dost thou forget
And I on the point of death?
Wilt thou ignore my prayer
Or wilt thou make known
Who thou art?
Thou mayest be what I thought,
Yet perchance thou art a phantom,
A thing that causes fear.
Oh, if I might know!
Oh, if it could be revealed!
Thou who made me out of earth,
And of clay formed me.
Oh look upon me!
Who art thou, O Creator?
Now I am very old.

(Peruvian, date unknown)

For a Happy Death

Holy Virgin,
I beg of you,
when my soul shall depart from my body,
be pleased to meet and receive it.

Mary,
do not refuse me then the grace
of being sustained by your sweet presence.
Be for me the ladder and the way to heaven,
and finally assure me of pardon and eternal rest.

(St. Bonaventure, 1221–74)

The Moment of Death

Come, my Savior, comfort my soul!
Make me steadfast in my love for you,
So that my love never falters.
When the moment of my death approaches,
Take from me any fear or grief;
Rather let me rejoice and be glad
That soon I shall enter your presence.
My mind is ablaze with love for you,
And my heart burns with desire to see you.
Therefore I endure earthly poverty,
And I despise earthly dignity,
Knowing that in heaven alone
Shall I find true wealth and true glory.

(Richard Rolle, c. 1300–49)

On One's Deathbed

O Holy Trinity, and O Morning Star,
O Scion from Royal David sprung,
Thy dear child Jesus, earnestly implore
To protect me on my journey home.

(Gaelic, date unknown)

Before Death

O Jesus Christ, O King of Grace,
Creator of Earth and of Paradise,
Thy blood the Tree of the Passion has laved
That I from eternal death should be saved.

I have ill repaid Thee during my life,
Reopening Thy wounds by my manifold sins,
Forgetting 'twas Thou Who gavest me health,
My daily bread, my herds, my wealth.

What use to me now my worldly store?
My friends, companions, kindred dear?
My warrant is signed and Death is calling,
And without Thy pardon to Hell I'm falling.

O God, Thou art the almighty Father,
Give me time to make my will,
My wealth on the poor like dew I'll spend,
And a perfume of praise to Thee shall ascend.

(Gaelic, date unknown)

For a Happy Death

Jesus, Mary and Joseph, I give you my heart and my soul.

Jesus, Mary and Joseph, assist me in my last agony.

Jesus, Mary and Joseph may I breathe forth my soul in peace with you.

(Christian, modern)

Death Song

Is there anyone who
>would weep for me?
My wife
>would weep for me.

(Chippewa, date unknown)

I Shall Never Disappear

I am intoxicated, I weep, I grieve,
I think, I speak,
within myself I discover this:
indeed, I shall never die,
indeed, I shall never disappear.
There where there is no death,
there where death is overcome,
let me go there.
Indeed I shall never die,
indeed, I shall never disappear.

(Nezahualcoyotl, a Nahuatl sage,
1402–72)

No Fear

*I*n heaven there is no fear—you are not there, [and] nobody is struck with fear because of old age. Having transcended both hunger and thirst and crossed over sorrow, one rejoices in the heavenly world.

(Katha Upanishad, I.i.12)

The Question

The savor of wandering in the
    ocean of deathless life has rid
    me of all my asking:
As the tree is in the seed, so all diseases
    are in this asking.

(Kabir, 1450?–1518)

What Will Thou Offer?

On the day when death will knock at thy door what wilt thou offer to him?

Oh, I will set before my guest the full vessel of my life—I will never let him go with empty hands.

All the sweet vintage of all my autumn days and summer nights, all the earnings and gleanings of my busy life will I place before him at the close of my days when death will knock at my door.

(Rabindranath Tagore, 1861–1941)

A Prayer in the Prospect of Death

O thou unknown, Almighty Cause
    Of all my hope and fear!
In whose dread presence, ere an hour,
    Perhaps I must appear!

If I have wandered in those paths
    Of life I ought to shun,
As something, loudly, in my breast,
    Remonstrates I have done;

Thou knowest that Thou hast formed me
    With passions wild and strong;
And listening to their witching voice
    Has often led me wrong.

Where human weakness has come short,
    Or frailty stepped aside,
Do Thou, All-Good!—for such Thou art,—
    In shades of darkness hide.

Where with intention I have erred,
    No other plea I have,
But, Thou art good; and Goodness still
    Delighteth to forgive.

(Robert Burns, 1759–96)

Parting Song

Farewell, O friends! for I am leaving you, O friends! *a ye ha a, a ye ya ha, aye!*

O friends! do not take it too much to heart that I am leaving you, O friends! *a ye ya ha a . . .*

O brothers! do not take it too much to heart that I am leaving you, O friends, *a ye ya ha . . .*

O sisters! do not feel sorrowful because I am leaving you, O sisters, *a ye ya ha . . .*

I was told by the one who takes care of me that I shall not stay away long, that I shall come back to you, O friends! *a ye ya ha . . .*

I mean, O friends! that you shall not feel too sorrowful when I leave you, O friends! *a ye ya ha a, a ye ha ha, aye a!*

(Sung by Ts'esquane, a Kwakiutl, on his deathbed, date unknown)

Lamentation

1.

I lift my voice in wailing, I am afflicted, as I remember that we must leave the beautiful flowers, the noble songs; let us enjoy ourselves for a while, let us sing, for we must depart forever, we are to be destroyed in our dwelling place.

2.

It is indeed known to our friends how it pains and angers me that never again can they be born, never again be young on this earth.

3.

Yet a little while with them here, then nevermore shall I be with them, nevermore enjoy them, nevermore know them.

4.

Where shall my soul dwell? Where is my home? Where shall be my house? I am miserable on earth.

5.

We take, we unwind the jewels, the blue flowers are woven over the yellow ones, that we may give them to the children.

6.

Let my soul be draped in various flowers; let it be intoxicated by them; for soon I must weeping go before the face of our Mother.

(Aztec, date unknown)

The School of Earth

*H*elp me to understand, Lord, that this earth is only the place where Thou art sending me to school. By and by graduating time will come and I shall hear Thee say, "Well done." I shall know that the work was not very well done. Only a heart of infinite love could call it that—as a mother might say tender words over a child's imperfect attempts. But Thou wilt say it, even to me. So, help me to be faithful and diligent and patient, till that day when the creature also shall be delivered into the glorious liberty of the children of God.

(Lucy Rider Meyer, modern)

Crossing the Bar

Sunset and evening star,
    And one clear call for me!
And may there be no moaning of the bar,
    When I put out to sea,

But such a tide as moving seems asleep,
    Too full for sound and foam,
When that which drew from out the boundless deep
    Turns again home.

Twilight and evening bell,
    And after that the dark!
And may there be no sadness of farewell,
    When I embark;

For though from out our borne of Time and Place
    The flood may bear me far,
I hope to see my Pilot face to face
    When I have crossed the bar.

(Alfred, Lord Tennyson, 1809–92)

Heaven

Think of—
Stepping on shore, and finding it Heaven!
Of taking hold of a hand, and finding it God's hand.
Of breathing a new air, and finding it celestial air.
Of feeling invigorated, and finding it immortality.
Of passing from storm and tempest to an unbroken calm.
Of waking up, and finding it Home.

(Author and date unknown)

A Voice from Afar

Weep not for me;—
Be blithe as wont, nor tinge with gloom
The stream of love that circles home,
    Light hearts and free!
Joy in the gifts Heaven's bounty lends;
Nor miss my face, dear friends!

    I still am near;—
Watching the smiles I prized on earth,
Your converse mild, your blameless mirth;
    Now too I hear
Of whispered sounds the tale complete,
Low prayers, and musings sweet.

    A sea before
The Throne is spread;—its pure still glass
Pictures all earth scenes as they pass,
    We, on its shore,
Share, in the bosom of our rest,
God's Knowledge, and are blest.

(Author and date unknown)

The Soul's Flight

What is this rapture of my eager soul?
     Where are those weeping ones about my bed?
     Am I on earth, or numbered with the dead?
And how, in pain till now, am I made whole?
Who are those beings, under whose control,
     I upward speed, borne by their wings outspread?
     What is this light and music round me shed?
Has earth receded, and is heaven my goal?
And what are those bright thronging shapes around?
     Do I not know them, as they beckon me?
     Tell me, my Guardians, all this mystery.
Yes, thou dear soul, with hymns of holy sound,
     Thy loved and lost to heaven do welcome thee,
Thine are they now, for all eternity.

(Author and date unknown)

The Remembrance of Those Who Sleep

Our sleeping dead, O Lord, are gone to Thee,
    To be for evermore in tranquil rest;
    Grant that, O Lord, we may with them be blest,
And with them, all Thy endless glory see.
O ever living, loving God, set free
    Our souls from every vain and worthless quest;
    To be with Thee, be that our sole behest;
With Thee in time, as in eternity:
Then with our dead shall we be blest indeed,
    And with them live in heaven, while here below;
    And with them too, in heavenly rapture grow;
For, while on earth, we shall from earth be freed,
    And all our life will be a path to go
    Where we, with them, Thy joy shall ever know.

(Author and date unknown)

Solace in Sorrow

Some solace for my sorrow,
    Some respite in my woe,
Some light in the to-morrow,
    Through which my path must go;
Such, Lord, I ask from Thy dear hand,
Teach me to hear, and understand.

In pain and grief I languish,
    And bitter tears I weep,
My heart is rent with anguish,
    For mine in death who sleep:
O send me comfort from above,
And make me never doubt Thy love.

O mourning soul forget not,
    That I for thee can weep,
Although I death thine are not,
    But only rest in sleep:
Like Lazarus, my voice they'll hear,
Then grieve not, doubt not, do not fear.

Ah Lord! I'll try to bear my loss,
I know with thee they live,
But help me, Lord, to bear my cross,
And comfort daily give.

My child, when in that better land
Then shalt thou know, and understand.

(Author and date unknown)

III

Prayers to Honor the Dead

Prayer for a Dead Friend

I feel strange, Lord,
because while I was sitting here
quietly reading the papers,
someone very close to me
was lying in an antiseptic room.
I didn't even know
that part of me was being cut off,
the precious part which was my friend,
so that now just half of me is alive,
and the other half
has slipped away into Your care.
And what can I do?
Heal myself, I guess:
close over the gaping wound of separation
and prepare for a new start.
Yet that's not all
I only now begin to realize
that my friend still lives in me,
in my memory,
in my feelings.
I must keep these feelings alive,
because if I don't,
then something beautiful
will truly have vanished from the earth.

(Max Pauli, modern)

Tattered Garment

Sing thou no plaintive lay
When my earthly remnant dies,
Nor let ashes tell thy tears where it lies.
Oh, blow my tattered garment's dust away!

Of dust clean-washed,
The hidden Gold beneath will show
Itself anew, all brightly brushed,
And shine somewhere with wisdom's glow.

It waits with luring luster
For the wandering Home-lorn soul—
To show the path, with lightning glimmer,
From darkness to the Goal.

(Paramahansa Yogananda, 1893–1952)

Prayer for the Dead

O Lord, our savior,
in your infinite mercy
grant the remission of all his/her sins
to the soul of [name],
who has departed this world.

Grant him/her your grace
that he/she may enter the gate of heaven.
May the departed soul find eternal solace
in the realm of the spirit,
where divine justice is complete.

Let the wonderful light of Johrei
shine forth in its purifying power
to save all souls from hell's damnation.

May this departed soul know salvation
in the realm of the spirit
and find never-ending joy
in union with the divine.
Hear our prayer, O Lord.

(Johrei, Japanese, modern)

Song for the Dead

Soul of the dead! depart; take thou the path—
The ancient path—by which our ancestors
Have gone before thee; thou shalt look upon
The two kings, mighty Varuna and Yama,
Delighting in oblations; thou shalt meet
The Fathers and receive the recompense
Of all thy stored-up offerings above.
Leave thou thy sin and imperfection here;
Return unto thy home once more; assume
A glorious form. By an auspicious path
Hasten to pass the four-eyed brindled dogs—
The two road-guarding sons of Sarama;
Advance to meet the Fathers who, with hearts
Kindly disposed towards thee, dwell in bliss
With Yama; and do thou, O mighty god,
Intrust him to thy guards to bring him to thee,
And grant him health and happiness eternal.

(Rig-Veda, X.14.7–11)

Lamentation

It is he, it is he,
The person with the spirit of an owl;
It is he, it is he,
The person with the spirit of an owl;
It is he, it is he.

All the manitous are weeping,
Because I go around weeping,
Because I go around weeping,
All the manitous are weeping.

The sky will weep,
The sky,
At the end of the earth;
The sky will weep.

(Fox, Native American tribe,
date unknown)

For a Child

O loving Jesus, who didst take little children unto thine arms to bless them; we believe that thou hast received the child now hidden from our sight. Thou lovedst him better than we loved him. Thou knewest what was best for him better than we knew. Thou willest, in thy love, that he should be with thee where thou art. We ask thee, O our Savior, to have mercy on us who remain. Make all thy children to know how short and uncertain their time is. May they learn to love thee in obedience and innocence, that so, when thou callest them away, their eyes may see the King in his beauty, and their voices join in the songs of those who praise thee day and night in thy temple. And unto thee, O blessed Lord Jesus, with the Father and the Holy Spirit shall be glory forever and ever.

(Christian, date unknown)

Farewell to the Warriors

Come
    it is time for you to depart
We are going on a long journey.

(Chippewa, date unknown)

Midé Burial Song

Neniwá
    let us stand
    and you shall see
    my body
    as I desire.

(Midé, date unknown)

Receive the Dead

Open thy arms, O earth, receive the dead
With gentle pressure and with loving welcome.
Enshroud him tenderly, e'en as a mother
Folds her soft vestment round the child she loves.

(Rig-Veda, X.18.11)

After a Death

O God, the God of the spirits of all flesh, in whose embrace all creatures live, in whatsoever world or condition they be: we beseech thee for him whose name and dwelling-place and every need thou knowest. Grant him light and rest, peace and refreshment, joy and consolation in Paradise, in the companionship of saints in the presence of Christ, and in the folds of thy great mercy. Grant that his life may unfold itself in thy sight, and find a sweet employment in the spacious fields of eternity. Mercifully keep us from every act here which may mar the fullness of the joy of meeting when the end of our days on earth has come, and pardon whatever is amiss in this our prayer, which we offer in the name of Christ our Lord and Savior.

(Christian, date unknown)

A Speech to the Dead

Now this day you have ceased to see daylight.

Think only of what is good.

Do not think of anything uselessly.

You must think all the time of what is good.

You will go and live with our nephew.

And do not think evil towards these your relatives

When you start to leave them this day you must not think backwards of
them with regret.

And do not think of looking back at them.

And do not feel badly because you have lost sight of this daylight.

This does not happen today to you alone, so that you thus be alone when
you die.

Bless the people so that they may not be sick.

This is what you will do.

You must merely bless them so that they may live as mortals here.

You must always think kindly.

Today is the last time I shall speak to you.

Now I shall cease speaking to you, my relative.

(Fox, date unknown)

Receive the Souls

Receive, O Lord, in tranquillity and peace, the souls of thy servants who, out of this present life, have departed unto thee. Grant them rest and place them in the habitations of light, the abodes of blessed spirits. Give them the life that knoweth not age, good things that pass not away; through Jesus Christ our Lord.

(St. Ignatius, second century)

For Those Who Mourn

*H*ave compassion, O most merciful Lord, on all who are mourning for those dear to them, and all who are lonely and desolate. Be thou their Comforter and Friend; give them such earthly solace as thou seest to be best for them; and bringing them to the fuller knowledge of thy love, do thou wipe away all their tears; for the sake of Jesus Christ our Lord.

(Christian, date unknown)

Death of a Sister

*B*ehold, oh, my sister! you have been deprived of the sight of your bodily self in the light of this day. Verily, as you go from this place and walk along the course of your way, it shall be with a feeling of peace in your heart; so shall it be as you go to Chibiabos [ruler of the land of the dead]. Look not behind you. Strive not to behold your parents and those that are your brothers and sisters. Verily, shall you say to Chibiabos: "This is the message I convey from those whom I have left disconsolate; long life is what they ask of you." You shall say to Chibiabos: "That they may live the full span of life given to man, is what they beg of you."

(Fox, date unknown)

Death of a Son

My son, listen once more to the words of your mother. You were brought into life with her pains. You were nourished with her life. She has attempted to be faithful in raising you up. When you were young she loved you as her life. Your presence has been a source of great joy to her. Upon you she depended for support and comfort in her declining days. She had always expected to gain the end of the path of life before you. But you have outstripped her, and gone before her. Our great and wise creator has ordered it thus. By his will I am left to taste more of the miseries of this world. Your friends and relatives have gathered about your body, to look upon you for the last time. They mourn, as with one mind, your departure from among us. We, too, have but a few days more, and our journey shall be ended. We part now, and you are conveyed from our sight. But we shall soon meet again, and shall again look upon each other. Then we shall part no more. Our maker has called you to his home. Thither we will follow. *Na-ho!*

(Iroquois, date unknown)

Upon a Lady That Died in Childbed, and Left a Daughter Behind Her

As Gilly flowers do but stay
To blow, and seed, and so away;
So you sweet Lady (sweet as May)
The garden's-glory liv'd a while,
To lend the world your scent and smile.
But when your own faire print was set
Once in a Virgin Flosculet,
(Sweet as your selfe, and newly blown)
To give that life, resign'd your own:
But so, as still the mother's power
Lives in the pretty Lady-flower.

(Robert Herrick, 1591–1674)

The Burial of an Infant

Blest infant bud, whose blossom-life
Did only look about, and fall
Wearied out in a harmless strife
Of tears, and milk, the food of all;

Sweetly didst thou expire: thy soul
Flew home unstain'd by his new kind;
For ere thou knew'st how to be foul,
Death wean'd thee from the world, and sin.

Softly rest all thy virgin-crumbs
Lapt in the sweets of thy young breath,
Expecting till thy Savior comes
To dress them, and unswaddle death!

(Henry Vaughan, 1622–95)

The Mother's Dream

I'd a dream to-night
As I fell asleep,
Oh! The touching sight
Makes me still to weep:
Of my little lad,
Gone to leave me sad,
Aye, the child I had,
But was not to keep.

As in heaven high,
I my child did seek,
There, in train, came by
Children fair and meek,
Each in lily-white,
With a lamp alight;
Each was clear to sight,
But they did not speak.

Then, a little sad,
Came my child in turn,
But the lamp he had,
Oh! it did not burn;
He, to clear my doubt,
Said, half turn'd about,
'Your tears put it out;
Mother, never mourn.'

(William Barnes, 1801–86)

Holy Innocents Day

They scarcely waked before they slept,
    They scarcely wept before they laughed;
    They drank indeed death's bitter draught,
But all its bitterest dregs were kept
And drained by Mothers while they wept.

From Heaven the speechless Infants speak:
    Weep not (they say), our Mothers dear,
    For swords nor sorrows come not here.
Now we are strong who were so weak,
And all is ours we could not seek.

We bloom among the blooming flowers,
    We sing among the singing birds;
    Wisdom we have who wanted words:
Here morning knows not evening hours,
All's rainbows here without the showers.

And softer than our Mother's breast,
    And closer than our Mother's arm,
    Is here the Love that keeps us warm
And broods above our happy nest.
Dear Mothers, come: for Heaven is best.

(Christina G. Rossetti, 1830–95)

Love Song of the Dead

You are hard-hearted against me, my dear,
ha ha ye ya ha ha!
You are cruel against me, my dear,
ha ha ye ya ha ha!
For I am tired of waiting for you to come here, my dear,
ha ha ye ya ha ha!
Now I shall cry differently on your account, my dear,
ha ha ye ya ha ha!
Ah, I shall go down to the lower world, there I shall
cry for you, my dear,
ha ha ye ya ha ha!

(Kwakiutl, date unknown)

Mourning Song of Other-Water

My younger brother has brought me a great joy of laughter.
If I knew the way the spirits go, I would go right to him.

(Tlingit, date unknown)

For a Child That Died

Here she lies, a pretty bud,
Lately made of flesh and blood:
Who, as soone, fell fast asleep,
As her little eyes did peep.
Give her strewings; but not stir
The earth, that lightly covers her.

(Robert Herrick, 1591–1674)

For the Dying

We commend unto Thee all those about to depart this life, beseeching Thee to grant unto them the spirit of tranquillity and trustfulness. May they put their hope in Thee and having passed through the valley of the shadow in peace, may they enter into the rest that remaineth for the people of God; through Jesus Christ our Lord.

(Professor Knight, nineteenth century)

The Death-Bed

We watch'd her breathing through the
    night,
    Her breathing soft and low,
As in her breast the wave of life
    Kept heaving to and fro.

So silently we seem'd to speak,
    So slowly moved about,
As we had lent her half our powers
    To eke her living out.

Our very hopes belied our fears,
    Our fears our hopes belied—
We thought her dying when she slept,
    And sleeping when she died.

For when the morn came dim and sad
    And chill with early showers,
Her quiet eyelids closed—she had
Another morn than ours.

(Thomas Hood, 1799–1845)

Into Paradise

May the Angels lead him into Paradise.

May the Martyrs receive him at his coming and take him to Jerusalem, the Holy City.

May the Choirs of the Angels receive him,
and may he, with the once poor Lazarus, have rest everlasting.

(The Roman Ritual)

In Mourning

O gracious Father, enable us Thy servants to bow before Thee in humble submission to Thy Divine appointment. Draw us, we pray Thee, unto Thyself, that while we mourn the loss of him we have so much loved, we may obtain consolation in the fuller knowledge of that love of Thine which at the first provided for us so great an earthly blessing, and is effectual to supply the place of every gift which Thy wisdom removes; and grant us, when this life of trial is ended, to find with him who has been taken from us a merciful judgment in the last day and a joyful entrance into Thy glory; through the merits of Jesus Christ our Lord.

(Rev. R. M. Benson, b. 1824)

A White Robe for a Child

*M*ay we become as this little child who now follows the Child Jesus, that Lamb of God, in a white robe whithersoever He goes; even so, Lord Jesus. Thou gavest him to us, Thou hast taken him from us. Blessed be the Name of the Lord. Blessed be our God for ever and ever.

(Rev. Martin J. Routh, b. 1755)

Life of Glory

O Lord, by Whom all souls live; we thank Thee for those whom Thy love has called from the life of trial to the life of rest. We trust them to Thy care; we pray Thee that by Thy grace we may be brought to enjoy with them the endless life of glory.

(Christian, date unknown)

A Deathbed

Her suffering ended with the day;
    Yet lived she at its close,
And breathed the long, long night away,
    In statue-like repose.

But when the sun, in all his state,
    Illumed the eastern skies,
She pass'd through glory's morning-gate,
    And walk'd in Paradise!

(James Aldrich, date unknown)

Wailing Song

The sky will weep,
The sky,
At the end of the earth;
The sky will weep.

(Fox, date unknown)

A Family's Deep Sorrow

Heavenly Father, hear our voice out of the deep sorrow which Thou in Thy mysterious wisdom hast brought upon us. We know that Thou art with us, and that whatsoever comest is a revelation of Thine unchanging love. Thou knowest what is best for us. Thy will be done. Thou gavest and Thou hast taken away, blessed be Thy Name. O keep our souls from all temptations of this hour of mourning, that we may neither sorrow as those without hope, nor lose our trust in Thee; but that the darker this earthly scene becometh the lighter may be our vision of that eternal world where all live before Thee. And grant that the remnant of this our family, O Lord, still being upon earth, may be steadfast in faith, joyful through hope, and rooted in love, and may so pass the waves of this troublesome world, that finally we may come to the land of everlasting life, there to reign with Thee, world without end, through Jesus Christ our Lord.

(Rev. L. Tuttiett, b. 1825)

For Divine Support

O Lord, our heavenly Father, without Whom all purposes are frustrate, all efforts are vain, grant us the assistance of the Holy Spirit, that we may not sorrow as those without hope, but may now return to the duties of our present life with humble confidence in Thy protection, and so govern our thoughts and actions that no business or work may ever withdraw our minds from Thee, but that in the changes of this life we may fix our hearts upon the reward which Thou hast promised to them that serve Thee, and that whatsoever things are true, whatsoever things are honest, whatsoever things are just, whatsoever things are pure, whatsoever things are lovely, whatsoever things are of good report, wherein there is virtue, wherein there is praise, we may think upon and do, and obtain mercy, consolation, and everlasting happiness. Grant this, O Lord, for the sake of Jesus Christ.

(Samuel Johnson, 1709–84)

Give Us Grace

*L*ord, do not permit our trials to be above our strength; and do Thou vouchsafe to be our strength and comfort in the time of trial. Give us grace to take in good part whatever shall befall us, and let our hearts acknowledge it to be the Lord's doing, and to come from Thy Providence, and not by chance. May we receive everything from Thy hand with patience and with joy; through Jesus Christ our Lord.

(Bishop Thomas Wilson, b. 1663)

A Month in Peace

A month among the happy living dead,
    What wonders must have flashed within thine eyes,
    Which see the glories of that paradise,
Whose splendors now before thy gaze are spread!
No more the weary earth, no more the dread
    Of loss or failure, or the sad surprise
    Of mortal sin; the way before thee lies
Straight to the feet of Him, our Risen Head.
As, on the earth, thou didst His Presence hail
    Upon His Altar Throne, in that sweet Feast,
Which told thee that His love should never fail;
So now, that Love which met thee at the Rail,
    Doth welcome thee, all earthly toil surceased,
    Thy dross all purged away, thy gold increased.

(Author and date unknown)

A Year at Rest

A year has past since last we saw thee here,
    A year! How long it seems to think thee dead,
    A year! Asleep in thy cold silent bed,
A year! And in each day for us a tear.
And yet, how oft we feel thy spirit near,
    Thy spirit which a blessing e'er doth shed,
    Whereby our inner souls are comforted,
As if thou still wert living here to cheer.
Yes, thou dost live, and in thy heavenly home,
    And, in the mirror of the crystal sea,
    Which spreads before all-seeing Deity,
Thou yet dost see us, as on earth we roam
    In all our sorrow and perplexity,
    And peace, thou bringest us, which tells of thee.

(Author and date unknown)

Epitaph Upon Husband and Wife Who Died and Were Buried Together

To these, whom death again did wed,
Their grave's the second marriage-bed,
For though the hand of fate could force
'Twixt soul and body a divorce,
It could not sever man and wife,
Because they both lived but one life.
Peace, good reader, do not weep
Peace, the lovers are asleep!
They (sweet turtles) folded lie,
In the last knot love could tie.
Let them sleep, let them sleep on,
Till this stormy night be gone,
And the eternal morrow dawn;
Then the curtains will be drawn,
And they will wake into a light
Whose day shall never end in night.

(Richard Crashaw, 1612–49)

IV

Prayers for Trying Times

If I May Hold Your Hand

As the rain hides the stars,
as the autumn mist hides the hills,
as the clouds veil the blue of the sky,
so the dark happenings of my lot
hide the shining of your face from me.
Yet, if I may hold your hand in the darkness,
it is enough.
Since I know that, though I may stumble in my going,
You do not fall.

(Gaelic, date unknown)

I Asked for Bread

I asked for bread; God gave a stone instead.
Yet, while I pillowed there my weary head,
The angels made a ladder of my dreams,
Which upward to celestial mountains led.
And when I woke beneath the morning's beams,
Around my resting place fresh manna lay;
And, praising God, I went upon my way.
For I was fed.

God answers prayer; sometimes when hearts are weak,
He gives the very gifts believers seek.
But often faith must learn a deeper rest,
And trust God's silence when He does not speak;
For He whose name is Love will send the best.
Stars may burn out, nor mountain walls endure,
But God is true, His promises are sure
For those who seek.

(Author and date unknown)

In Time of Trial

All-holy Lady,
do not abandon me to the power of human beings.
Hear the plea of your servant
for I am oppressed by anguish
and find it difficult to resist the pressures of evil.
I have no defense
and I do not know where to flee.
I am assailed on all sides
and I find no consolation except in you.
Queen of the world,
hope and protection of the faithful,
do not despise my petition
but grant me what I need.

(Byzantine Liturgy)

I Bow My Troubled Soul

My God and King! To thee
I bow my knee,
I bow my troubled soul, and greet
With my foul heart thy holy feet.
Cast it, or tread it! It shall do
Even what thou wilt, and praise thee too.

My God, could I weep blood,
Gladly I would;
Of if thou wilt give me that art,
Which through the eyes pours out the heart,
I will exhaust it all, and make
Myself all tears, a weeping lake.

O! 'tis an easy thing
To write and sing;
But to write true, unfeigned verse
Is very hard! O God, disperse
These weights, and give my spirit leave
To act as well as to conceive!

O my God, hear my cry;
Or let me die!

(Henry Vaughan, 1622–95)

A Steadfast, Upright Heart

Give me, O Lord, a steadfast heart,
   which no unworthy affection may drag downwards;
give me an unconquered heart,
   which no tribulation can wear out;
give me an upright heart,
   which no unworthy purpose may tempt aside.

(St. Thomas Aquinas, 1225–74)

I Am Walking

Toward calm and shady places
I am walking
on the earth.

(Chippewa, date unknown)

For Deprivation

*L*ord, I thank you that in your love you have taken from me all earthly
riches, and that now you clothe and feed me through the generosity
of others.

(Mechtild of Magdeburg, 1210–80)

When Gray Clouds Gather

When we see dark gray clouds forming in the sky, we fear a mighty storm. In the same way when we see the darkness of our sin, we fear the storm of your wrath. But just as in truth rain brings new life to the earth, so you rain down mercy on our sinful souls, bringing forgiveness and peace. Be to us always like a mighty storm, raining down upon us the abundant waters of your mercy.

(Gilbert of Hoyland, died c. 1170)

As God Will

Pain's furnace heat within me quivers,
    God's breath upon the flame doth blow,
And every part within me shivers
    And quivers in the fiery glow.
Yet say I, trusting: "As God will,"
And in His hottest fires hold still.

He kindles for my profit purely
    Affliction's glowing, fiery brand;
And every blow He deals me, surely,
    Is given by a master hand.
So say I, hoping: "As God will,"
And in His hottest fires hold still.

Why should I murmur, for thus the sorrow
    Only longer-lived would be.
Peace may come—yes, will—tomorrow,
    When God has done His work in me.
So say I, praying: "As God will,"
And in His hottest fires hold still.

(Author and date unknown)

Lord, Grant Us Calm

Lord, grant us calm, if calm can set forth Thee;
Or tempest, if a tempest set Thee forth:
Wind from the east or west or south or north,—
Or congelation of a silent sea,
With stillness of each tremulous aspen tree.

Still let fruit fall, or hang upon the tree;
Still let the east and west, the south and north,
Curb in their winds—or plough a thundering sea:
Still let the earth abide to set Thee forth,
Or vanish like a smoke to set forth Thee.

(Christina G. Rossetti, 1830–95)

When in Trouble

O Lord Jesus, our Savior and Friend, we pray Thee shelter us in all these troubles. Give us strength to bear them, and grant that we may never complain but try to bear our cross as Thou didst Thine for us, till Thou callest us to dwell with Thee for ever and ever.

(Christian, date unknown)

To Relieve Depression

*J*ust as day declines to evening, so often after some little pleasure my heart declines into depression. Everything seems dull, every action feels like a burden. If anyone speaks, I scarcely listen. If anyone knocks, I scarcely hear. My heart is as hard as flint. Then I go out into the field to meditate, to read the holy Scriptures, and I write down my deepest thoughts in a letter to you. And suddenly your grace, dear Jesus, shatters the darkness with daylight, lifts the burden, relieves the tension. Soon tears follow sighs, and heavenly joy floods over me with the tears.

(Aelred of Rievaulx, c. 1110–67)

In Time of Rain

We thank thee, Lord, for the glory of the late days and the excellent face of thy sun. We thank thee for good news received. We thank thee for the pleasures we have enjoyed and for those we have been able to confer. And now, when the clouds gather and the rain impends over the forest and our house, permit us not to be cast down. Let us not lose the savor of past mercies and past pleasures; but, like the voice of a bird singing in the rain, let grateful memory survive in the hour of darkness. If there be in front of us any painful duty, strengthen us with the grace of courage; if any act of mercy, teach us tenderness and patience.

(Robert Louis Stevenson, 1850–94)

The Ship of Life

Steer the ship of my life, good Lord, to your quiet harbor, where I can be safe from the storms of sin and conflict. Show me the course I should take. Renew in me the gift of discernment, so that I can always see the right direction in which I should go. And give me the strength and the courage to choose the right course, even when the sea is tough and the waves are high, knowing that through enduring hardship and danger in your name we shall find comfort and peace.

(Basil of Caesarea, c. 330–379)

For the Unjustly Accused

O Lord, strengthen and support, we entreat thee, all persons unjustly accused or misunderstood. Comfort them by the ever-present thought that thou knowest the whole truth, and wilt in thine own good time make their righteousness as clear as the light. Give them grace to pray for such as do them wrong, and hear and bless them when they pray, for the sake of Jesus Christ our Lord.

(Christina G. Rossetti, 1830–95)

In Time of Trouble

O sweetest Jesus, Thou art my protection and my strength in time of strife: Thou art my joy in time of prosperity. O vouchsafe relief to me in this difficulty.

(Gaelic, date unknown)

Prayer to Obtain Spiritual Help

O King of the Universe
Who early lightest the sun,
Who sendest heavy rains
And the crops that after them come:
For Thee I set down my faults,
To Thee I turn my face,
O Lord, do not permit me
To fall from the state of grace.

(Gaelic, date unknown)

Darkness Song

We wait in the darkness!
Come, all ye who listen,
Help in our night journey;
Now no sun is shining;
Now no star is glowing;
Come, show us the pathway;
The night is not friendly;
She closes her eyelids;
The moon has forgotten us,
We wait in the darkness!

(Iroquois, date unknown)

Sonnet to Illness

Sometimes God sets man aside for awhile
To take stock of life—where we are going.
Illness has a way of reducing style,
Shorning us to our original being.
It gives us time out to think and to say
Things we oft hurried by while we were well
Or note rules of health we seldom obey,
Our own bodies the true story could tell.
But now we are given a special time
To write new rules from the light of the sky.
We shall start again, create a new clime
One that will last until the day we die:
  All of our old ways we shall give the knife,
  Illness to us was our new lease on life.

(Rosemary C. Wilkinson, modern)

Bless the Earth

Bless to me, O God
The earth beneath my foot,
Bless to me, O God,
The path whereon I go.

(Gaelic, date unknown)

Fountain of Blessings

O God, Who art the unsearchable abyss of peace, the ineffable sea of love, the fountain of blessings and the bestower of affection, Who sendest peace to those that receive it; open to us this day the sea of Thy love, and water us with plenteous streams from the riches of Thy grace. Make us children of quietness, and heirs of peace. Enkindle in us the fire of Thy love; strengthen our weakness by Thy power; bind us closely to Thee and to each other in one firm and indissoluble bond of unity.

(Syrian Clementine Liturgy)

Somehow Strength Lasted

Somehow strength lasted through the day,
Hope joined with courage in the way;
The feet still kept the uphill road,
The shoulders did not drop their load,
And unseen power sustained the heart
When flesh and will failed in their part,
    While God gave light
    By day and night,
And also grace to bear the smart.
    For this give thanks.

(Author and date unknown)

After the Storm

Help us, dear Savior! The Comforter of those who seek, the Steadfast Friend of those who, through sorrow, pain, or for any other cause, come to Thee for help and direction. May we so shape our course in this world of shadow and sunshine that we may be blessed with peace and hope after the storms, of trials and unhappiness. May our lives manifest Thy goodness to us, and our hearts radiate love, hope and trust, so that others may rejoice with us and be led to the source of all comfort. We ask it in the name of all those who need Thy peace and joy to sustain them on Life's journey.

(Elinor Cochrane Stewart, modern)

For Comfort

*A*lmighty and everlasting God, the Comfort of the sad, the Strength of sufferers, let the prayers of those that cry out of any tribulation come unto thee, that all may rejoice to find that thy mercy is present with them in their afflictions, through Jesus Christ our Lord.

(Gelasian Sacramentary, 492–496)

Made Perfect Through Suffering

I bless thee, Lord, for sorrows sent
To break my dream of human power;
For now my shallow cistern's spent,
I find thy founts, and thirst no more.

I take thy hand and fears grow still;
Behold thy face and doubts remove;
Who would not yield his wavering will
To perfect Truth and boundless Love?

That Love this restless soul doth teach
The strength of thine eternal calm;
And tune its sad and broken speech,
To join, on earth, the angels' psalm.

Oh, be it patient in thy hands,
And drawn, through each mysterious hour,
To service of thy pure commands,
The narrow way to Love and Power.

(Samuel Johnson, 1709–84)

Be Near Me When My Light Is Low

Be near me when my light is low;
    When the blood creeps, and the nerves prick
    And tingle; and the heart is sick,
And all the wheels of Being slow.

Be near me when the sensuous frame
    Is racked with pangs that conquer trust;
    And Time, a maniac scattering dust,
And Life, a Fury slinging flame.

Be near me when my faith is dry,
    And when the flies of latter spring,
    And lay their eggs, and sting and sing,
And weave their petty cells, and die.

Be near me when I fade away,
    To point the term of human strife,
    And, on the low dark verge of life,
The twilight of eternal day.

(Alfred, Lord Tennyson, 1809–92)

God, Make Me Brave

God, make me brave for life: oh, braver than this.
Let me straighten after pain, as a tree straightens after the rain,
Shining and lovely again.
God, make me brave for life; much braver than this.
As the blown grass lifts, let me rise
From sorrow with quiet eyes,
Knowing Thy ways is wise.
God, make me brave, life brings
Such blinding things.
Help me to keep my sight;
Help me to see aright
That out of dark comes light.

(Author and date unknown)

The Peace of Pain

There is a peace which no men know
Save those whom suffering hath laid low,—
    The peace of pain.

A strength, which only comes to those
Who've borne defeat—greater, God knows,
    Than victory.

A happiness which comes at last,
After all happiness seems past,—
    The joy of peace.

(Author and date unknown)

In Times of Anxiety

O God, Who makest cheerfulness the companion of strength, but apt to take wings in time of sorrow, we humbly beseech Thee that if, in Thy sovereign wisdom, Thou sendest weakness, yet for Thy mercy's sake deny us not the comfort of patience. Lay not more upon us, O heavenly Father, than Thou wilt enable us to bear; and since the fretfulness of our spirits is more hurtful than the heaviness of our burden, grant us that heavenly calmness which comes of owning Thy hand in all things, and patience in the trust that Thou doest all things well; through Jesus Christ.

(Rev. Rowland Williams, b. 1818)

St. Teresa's Bookmark

Let nothing disturb thee.
Let nothing affright thee.
All things are passing.
Patience obtains all things.
He who has God has everything.
God alone suffices.

(St. Teresa of Avila, 1515–82)

Eternal Calm

Wearied by the conflict of life, worn by the burden of the day, we seek Thee as our resting-place. May Thy eternal calm descend upon our troubled spirits and give us all Thy peace. Amid the treacherous sands of time Thou standest still, the Rock of Ages. In life's desert places Thou, O Christ, art a spring whose waters never fail; hear us, we beseech Thee, O Lord Christ.

(Rev. Dr. Orchard, b. 1877)

Strengthen Us

*M*ost merciful God, the Helper of all men, so strengthen us by Thy power that our sorrow may be turned into joy, and we may continually glorify Thy holy Name; through Jesus Christ our Lord.

(Sarum Breviary, 1085)

Two Outlooks

I have a bridge within my heart,
    Known as the Bridge of Sighs;
It stretches from life's sunny part,
    To where its darkness lies.

And when upon this bridge I stand,
    To watch life's tide below,
Sad thoughts come from the shadowy land,
    And darken all its flow.

Then, as it winds its way along
    To sorrow's bitter sea,
Oh! mournful is the spirit song
    That upward floats to me.

A song which breathes of blessings dead,
    Of friends and friendships flown;
And pleasures gone! their distant tread
    Now to an echo grown.

I have a bridge within my heart,
    Known as the Bridge of Faith;
It spans, by a mysterious art,
    The streams of life and death.

And when upon that bridge I stand,
    To watch the tide below,
Sweet thoughts come from the sunny land,
    And brighten all below.

A song of blessings never sere,
    Of love beyond compare;
Of pleasures flowed from troublings here,
    To rise serenely there.

And, hearing thus, a peace divine
    Soon shuts each sorrow out;
And all is hopeful and benign,
    Where all was fear and doubt.

(Author and date unknown)

V

*P*rayers for
*F*orgiveness
and *C*ompassion

Forgiveness

All that we ought to have thought and have not thought,
All that we ought to have said, and have not said,
All that we ought to have done, and have not done;

All that we ought not to have thought, and yet have thought,
All that we ought not to have spoken, and yet have spoken,
All that we ought not to have done, and yet have done;
For thoughts, words and works, pray we, O God, for forgiveness.

(Persian, date unknown)

Who, Me?

I need to be forgiven, Lord
So many times a day,
So often do I slip and fall,
Be merciful, I pray!
And help me not be critical
When others' faults I see;
For so many times, my Lord,
The same faults are in me.

(Author and date unknown)

In Times of Darkness

Grant unto us, Almighty God, in all time of sore distress, the comfort of the forgiveness of our sins. In time of darkness give us blessed hope, in time of sickness of body give us quiet courage; and when the heart is bowed down, and the soul is very heavy, and life is a burden, and pleasure a weariness, and the sun is too bright, and life too mirthful, then may that Spirit, the Spirit of the Comforter, come upon us, and after our darkness may there be the clear shining of the heavenly light; that so, being uplifted again by Thy mercy, we may pass on through this mortal life with quiet courage, patient hope, and unshaken trust, hoping through Thy loving-kindness and tender mercy to be delivered from death into the large life of the eternal years. Hear us through Thy mercy, through Jesus Christ our Lord.

(Rev. George Dawson, 1821–76)

Help Us, O Lord

Help us, O Lord, with patient love to bear
    Each other's faults; to suffer with true meekness;
Help us each other's joys and griefs to share,
    But let us turn to Thee alone in weakness.

(Prayer used by John Quincy Adams, 1767–1848)

For Enemies

O Thou, who hast directed us to overcome evil with good, and hast expressly commanded our prayers for them that persecute us, and despitefully use us, pardon and bless all that speak evil of me, all that have hated me with or without a cause: some of them perhaps even for my own good will, for speaking distasteful truth or doing necessary justice: but whatever the occasion or the offense may have been, which, if given on my part, I entreat Thee, and them, to forgive: have the same mercy, O Lord, on all mine enemies, as on myself: and bring them, I beseech Thee, to Thy heavenly kingdom, as I hope and pray Thou wilt at length bring me.

(Abbie C. Morrow, modern)

Hold Forth Thy Light

O God our Father, hear me, who am trembling in this darkness, and stretch forth thy hand unto me; hold forth thy light before me; recall me from my wanderings; and, thou being my guide, may I be restored to myself and to thee.

(St. Augustine, 354–430)

Promise of Forgiveness

Almighty God, our heavenly Father, who of his great mercy hath promised forgiveness of sins to all those who with hearty repentance and true faith turn unto him; have mercy upon us; pardon and deliver us from all our sins; confirm and strengthen us in all goodness and bring us to everlasting life.

(Christian, date unknown)

Cleanse Us

O Lord our God, great, eternal, wonderful in glory, Who keepest covenant and promise for those that love Thee with their whole heart, Who art the life of all, the help of those that flee unto Thee, the hope of those who cry unto Thee. Cleanse us from our sins, and from every thought displeasing to Thy goodness, cleanse our souls and bodies, our hearts and consciences that with a pure heart and a clear mind, with perfect love and calm hope, we may venture confidently and fearlessly to pray unto Thee, through Jesus Christ our Lord.

(Coptic Liturgy of St. Basil, 370)

For Transformation of the Past

O love unspeakable and full of glory, whose majesty is not to destroy, but to save, save us from ourselves. Our past relentlessly pursues us. Days that we thought dead live over again; deeds that we deemed buried meet us on the way; be thou our defense, O our God.

Fill up that which our lives have left behind. Undo that which we have done amiss. Repair the places we have wasted, bind the hearts we have wounded. Dry the eyes which we have flooded. Make the evil we have done work for good, so that we ourselves would not know it.

Take up our yesterdays into thine own golden light and transfigure them there, that we may learn with joyful surprise how ever against our wills we were laboring together with thee; so shall our former selves find us no more.

(Christian, date unknown)

To Train Our Hearts

Help us, O Divine Lord of Life, to train our hearts, as servants of God, to mercy, kindness, humbleness of mind, long-suffering, forbearance, and gentleness. Give us the largeness and depth of character whereby we may forgive one another if any man have a quarrel against us, even as God, for Christ's sake, forgives us, so help us to forgive others. And above all things, give us love, which is the bond of perfectness, and may the peace of God dwell in our hearts.

(Christian, date unknown)

Forgive Hatred

As the first martyr prayed to thee for his murderers, O Lord, so we fall before thee and pray; forgive all who hate and maltreat us and let not one of them perish because of us, but may all be saved by thy grace, O God the all-bountiful.

(Eastern Church)

For Those in Need

O God, remember in thy mercy the poor and needy, the widow and the fatherless, the stranger and the friendless, the sick and the dying [and any such known to us whom we name in our heart before thee] and those who do not pray for themselves and who have none to pray for them. Relieve their needs, sanctify their sufferings, strengthen their weakness; and in due time bring them out of bondage into the glorious liberty of the sons of God.

(Christian, date unknown)

Have Compassion

*H*ave compassion, we beseech thee, O Lord, upon all those whose hearts are touched with sorrow, whose spirits are troubled or cast down within them. O Lord, remember those to whom the burdens of this life bring dimness or darkness of soul. Send them help from above, and have mercy on all who suffer in body or mind, from whatever cause. O Lord, have mercy on them continually.

(Christian, date unknown)

Give Thine Angels Charge

Before we go to rest we commit ourselves to thy care, O God our Father, beseeching thee through Christ our Lord to keep alive thy grace in our hearts. Watch thou, O Heavenly Father, with those who wake or watch or weep tonight and give thine angels charge over those who sleep. Tend those who are sick, rest those who are weary, soothe those who suffer, pity those in affliction; be near and bless those who are dying, and keep under thy holy care those who are dear to us.

(Christian, date unknown)

For Those Who Suffer

O thou who art Love, and who seest all the suffering, injustice and misery which reign in this world; look mercifully upon the poor, the oppressed, and all who are heavy laden with labor and sorrow. Fill our hearts with deep compassion for those who suffer, and hasten the coming of thy kingdom of justice and truth.

(Christian, date unknown)

Watch, O Lord

Watch, O Lord, with those who wake, or watch, or weep tonight,
and give Your angels and saints charge over those who sleep.
Tend Your sick ones, O Lord Christ.
Rest Your weary ones.
Bless Your dying ones.
Soothe Your suffering ones.
Pity Your afflicted ones.
Shield Your joyous ones,
and all for Your love's sake.

(St. Augustine, 354–430)

For the Lonely

O Lord, Thou lover of souls, in whose hand is the life of every living thing, we bring before Thee in our prayers all those who are lonely in the world. Thine they are, and none can pluck them out of Thy hand. In Thy pitiful mercy let our remembrance reach them and comfort their hearts.

(Christian, date unknown)

Dare I Pass By?

If I could see
A brother languishing in sore distress,
And I should turn and leave him comfortless,
    When I might be
A messenger of hope and happiness—
How could I ask to have that I denied
In my own hour of bitterness supplied?

    If I might share
A brother's load along the dusty way,
And I should turn and walk alone that day,
    How could I dare—
When in the evening watch I kneel to pray—
To ask for help to bear my pain and loss,
If I had heeded not my brother's cross?

(Author and date unknown)

Keeping Open Heart

My home is not so great,
    But open heart I keep;
The sorrows come to me,
    That they may sleep.

The little bread I have
    I share, and gladly pray
Tomorrow may give more,
    To give away.

Yet, in the dark sometimes
    The childish fear will haunt:
How long, how long, before
    I die of want?

But all the bread I have
    I share, and ever say,
Tomorrow shall bring more
    To give away.

(Author and date unknown)

The Noble New

Sing songs that none have sung,
Think thoughts that ne'er in brain have rung,
Walk in paths that none have trod,
Weep tears as none have shed for God,
Give peace to all to whom none other gave,
Claim him your own who's everywhere disclaimed.
Love all with love that none have felt, and brave
The battle of life with strength unchained.

(Paramahansa Yogananda, 1893–1952)

VI

*Prayers to Help
Us Remember
Who We Are*

From the Eternal Goodness

I know not what the future hath
Of marvel or surprise,
Assured alone that life and death
His mercy underlies.

And if my heart and flesh are weak
To bear an untried pain,
The bruised reed he will not break,
But strengthen and sustain.

No offering of my own I have,
Nor works my faith to prove;
I can but give the gifts he gave,
And plead his love for love.

And so beside the silent sea
I wait the muffled oar;
No harm from him can come to me
On ocean or on shore.

I know not where his islands lift
Their fronded palms in air;
I only know I cannot drift
Beyond his love and care.

(*John Greenleaf Whittier, 1807–92*)

My Music

My music
   reaches
   to the sky.

(Chippewa, date unknown)

Brother Sun, Sister Moon

Most high, omnipotent, righteous Lord, to you be all praise, glory, honor and blessing. To you alone are they due, and no man is worthy to mention you.

Praise be to you, my Lord, for all your creatures, above all Brother Sun, who gives us the light of day. He is beautiful and radiant with great splendour, and so is like you most high Lord.

Praise be to you, my Lord, for Sister Moon and the stars. In heaven you fashioned them, clear and precious and beautiful.

Praise be to you, my Lord, for Brother Wind, and for every kind of weather, cloudy or fair, stormy or serene, by which you cherish all that you have made.

Praise be to you, my Lord, for Sister Water, which is useful and humble and precious and pure.

Praise be to you, my Lord, for Brother Fire, by whom you lighten the night, for he is beautiful and playful and robust and strong.

Praise be to you, my Lord, for our Sister Earth, who sustains and governs us, and produces varied fruits with colored flowers and herbs.

Praise be to you, my Lord, for those who forgive sins in your love, and for those who bear sickness and tribulation.

Blessed are those who endure in peace, for by you, most high Lord, they shall be crowned.

Praise be to you, my Lord, for our Sister Bodily Death, from whom no living person can escape. Pity those who die in mortal sin.

Blessed are those who in death are found obedient to your most holy will, for death shall do them no harm.

Praise and bless my Lord, giving him thanks and serving him with great humility.

(St. Francis of Assisi, 1182?—1226)

A Grape, a Well, a Spark, a Seed

Lord, how much juice you can squeeze from a single grape.
How much water you can draw from a single well,
How great a fire you can kindle from a tiny spark.
How great a tree you can grow from a tiny seed,
My soul is so dry that by itself it cannot pray;
Yet you can squeeze from it the juice of a thousand prayers.
My soul is so parched that by itself it cannot love;
Yet you can draw from it boundless love for you and for my neighbor.
My soul is so cold that by itself it has no joy;
Yet you can light the fire of heavenly joy within me.
My soul is so feeble that by itself it has no faith;
Yet by your power my faith grows to a great height.
Thank you for prayer, for love, for joy, for faith;
Let me always be prayerful, loving, joyful, faithful.

(Guigo the Carthusian, d. 1188)

The Call

Come, my Way, my Truth, my Life;
Such a Way, as gives us breath:
Such a Truth, as ends all strife:
And such a Life, as killeth death.

Come, my Light, my Feast, my Strength:
Such a Light, as shows a feast:
Such a Feast, as mends in length;
Such a Strength, as makes his guest.

Come, my Joy, my Love, my Heart:
Such a Joy, as none can move:
Such a Wave, as none can part:
Such a Heart, as joys in love.

(George Herbert, 1593–1633)

Offering to the Creator

Creator! you who dwell at the ends of the earth unrivaled, you who gave being and power to men, saying: let this be man, and to women, saying: let this be woman! So saying, you made them, shaped them, gave them being. These you created; watch over them! Let them be safe and well, unharmed, living in peace. Where are you? Up in the sky? Or down below? In clouds? In storms? Hear me, answer me, acknowledge me, give us perpetual life, hold us forever within your hand. Receive this offering wherever you are. Creator!

(Inca, date unknown)

The Light That Gives Life

Holy Spirit, the life that gives life.
You are the cause of all movement;
You are the breath of all creatures;
You are the salve that purifies our souls;
You are the ointment that heals our wounds;
You are the fire that warms our hearts;
You are the light that guides our feet.
Let all the world praise you.

(Hildegard of Bingen, 1098–1179)

Our Need

O Lord,
never suffer us to think
that we can stand by ourselves,
and not need Thee.

(John Donne, 1572–1631)

Description of Himself

Who am I?
I live flying,
I compose hymns,
I sing the flowers:
butterflies of song.
They leap forth from within me,
my heart relishes them.
I have arrived among the people,
I have come down,
I, the bird of spring.
I have spread my wings over the earth
in the place of the flower-decked drums.
My song arises over the earth,
my song bursts out.

(Tlapalteuccitzin, a Nahuatl sage, date unknown)

All Things

All things are created by the Om;
    The love-form is His body.
He is without form, without quality, without decay:
Seek thou union with Him!
But that formless God takes a thousand forms in the eyes of His creatures:
He is pure and indestructible,
His form is infinite and fathomless,
He dances in rapture, and waves of form arise from His dance.
The body and the mind cannot contain themselves, when they are
    touched by His great joy.
He is immersed in all consciousness, all joys, and all sorrows;
He has no beginning and no end;
He holds all within His bliss.

(Kabir, 1450?–1518)

Food for Eternity

Thou, O my God, art ever new, though Thou art the most ancient. Thou alone art the food for eternity. I am to live for ever; not for a time—and I have no power over my being; I must live on, with intellect and consciousness for ever, in spite of myself. Without Thee eternity would be another name for eternal misery. In Thee alone have I that which can stay me up for ever; Thou alone art the food of my soul. Thou alone art inexhaustible, and ever offerest to me something new to know, something new to love. And so on for eternity I shall ever be a little child beginning to be taught the rudiments of Thy infinite Divine nature. For Thou art Thyself the seat and center of all good, and the only substance in this universe of shadows, and the heaven in which blessed spirits live and rejoice.

(Cardinal John Henry Newman, 1801–90)

For Brotherhood

*M*ay I be no man's enemy, and may I be the friend of that which is eternal and abides. May I never quarrel with those nearest me; and if I do, may I be reconciled quickly. May I never devise evil against any man; if any devise evil against me, may I escape uninjured and without the need of hurting him. May I love, seek, and attain only that which is good.

(Bishop Eusebius of Caesarea, 265–340)

For Nature

Almighty One, in the woods I am blessed. Happy everyone in the woods. Every tree speaks through thee. O God! What glory in the woodland! On the heights is peace—peace to serve him.

(Ludwig van Beethoven, 1770–1827)

Eternal Strength and Wisdom

Ere on my bed my limbs I lay,
It hath not been my use to pray
With moving lips or bended knees,
But silently, by slow degrees,
My spirit I to Love compose,
In humble trust mine eyelids close
With reverential resignation,
No wish conceived, no thought expressed,
Only a sense of supplication;
A sense all o'er my soul impressed
That I am weak, yet not unblest,
Since in me, round me, everywhere,
Eternal strength and wisdom are.

(Samuel Taylor Coleridge, 1772–1834)

Indian Prayer

Oh! Thou great mystery,
Creator of the universe,
Good and powerful as Thou art,
Whose powers are displayed in
The wonders of the sun and glories of the moon,
And the great foliage of the forest
And the great waters of the deep,
Sign of the four winds;
Whatever four corners of the earth that we may meet—
Let us be friends, pale face and red man,
And when we come to the end of that long trail,
And we step off into the happy hunting ground,
From which no hunter ever returns,
Let us not only have faith in Thee—Oh, thou great Mystery—
But faith in each other.
Oh! Thou Kitchi Manito, hear us!

(Chief Joseph Strongwolf, date unknown)

The Wise Seer Within

                              I will be
Light-hearted as a bird, and live with God.
I find Him in the bottom of my heart,
I hear continually His voice therein;
The little needle always knows the North,
The little bird remembereth his note,
And this wise Seer within me never errs.
I never taught it what it teaches me;
I only follow, when I act aright.

(Ralph Waldo Emerson, 1803–82)

To the Master-Builder

The windows of the place wherein I dwell
I will make beautiful. No garish light
Shall enter crudely; but with colors bright
And warm and throbbing I will weave a spell,
In rainbow harmony the theme to tell
Of sage and simple saint and noble knight,
Beggar and king who fought the gallant fight.

These will transfigure even my poor cell.
But when the shadows of the night begin,
And sifted sunlight falls no more on me,
May I have learned to light my lamp within;
So that the passing world may see
Still the same radiance, though with paler hue,
Of the sweet lives that help men to live true.

(Author and date unknown)

The Rainbow

My heart leaps up when I behold
    A Rainbow in the sky:
So was it when my life began;
So is it now I am a Man;
So be it when I shall grow old,
    Or let me die!
The Child is Father of the Man;
And I could wish my days to be
Bound each to each by natural piety.

(William Wordsworth, 1770–1850)

*I*nspiration

Your life is inspiration itself
from your heart radiates the oneness of all
from your thoughts creations spring,
You, are the inspiration for all there is.

(Joann Marie Everett, modern)

VII

*P*rayers of
*E*xaltation
and *H*appiness

The Call

Come, my Way, my Truth, my Life;
Such a Way, as gives us breath:
Such a Truth, as ends all strife:
And such a Life, as killeth death.

Come, my Light, my Feast, my Strength:
Such a Light, as shows a feast:
Such a Feast, as mends in length:
Such a Strength, as makes his guest.

Come, my Joy, my Love, my Heart:
Such a Joy, as none can move:
Such a Love, as none can part:
Such a Heart, as joys in love.

(George Herbert, 1593–1633)

Divine Providence

I implore thee, thou God,
I pray to thee during the night.
How are all people kept by thee all days?
And thou walkest in the midst of the grass,
I walk with thee;
When I sleep in the house I sleep with thee.
To thee I pray for food, and thou givest it to the people
And water to drink.

(Shilluk, Sudan, date unknown)

God's Glory

Lord, where can I find You?
Your glory fills the world.

Behold, I find You
Where the ploughman breaks the hard soil,
Where the quarrier explodes stone out of the hillside,
Where the miner digs metals out of the reluctant earth,
Where men and women earn their bread by the sweat of their brow,
Among the lonely and poor, the lowly and lost.
    In blazing heat and shattering storm, You are with them.

Behold, I find You
In the mind free to sail by its own star,
In words that spring from the depth of truth,
Where endeavor reaches undespairing for perfection,
Where the scientist toils to unravel the secrets of Your world,
Where the poet makes beauty out of words,
Wherever people struggle for freedom,
    Wherever noble deeds are done.

Behold, I find You
In the shouts of children merry at their play,
In the mother's lullaby, as she rocks her baby in the cradle,
In the sleep falling on his infant eyelids,
    And in the smile that dances on his sleeping lips.

Behold, I find You
When dawn comes up bearing golden gifts,
And in the fall of evening peace and rest from the Western sea.
In the current of life flowing day and night through all things,
Throbbing in my sinews and in the dust of the earth,
    In every leaf and flower.

Behold, I find You
In the wealth of joys that quickly fade,
In the life that from eternity dances in my blood,
In birth, which renews the generations continually,
    And in death knocking on the doors of life.

O my God,
Give me strength never to disown the poor,
Never before insolent might to bow the head.
Give me strength to raise my spirit high above daily trifles,
Lightly to bear my joys and sorrows,
And in love to surrender all my strength to Your will.

For great are Your gifts to me:
The sky and the light. This my flesh.
Life and the soul—
Treasures beyond price, treasures of life and of love.

(Jewish, modern)

We Return Thanks

We return thanks to our mother, the earth, which sustains us. We return thanks to the rivers and streams, which supply us with water. We return thanks to all herbs, which furnish medicines for the cure of our diseases. We return thanks to the corn, and to her sisters, the beans and squashes, which give us life. We return thanks to the bushes and trees, which provide us with fruit. We return thanks to the wind, which, moving the air, has banished diseases. We return thanks to the moon and stars, which have given to us their light when the sun was gone. We return thanks to our grandfather *Hé-no*, that he has protected his grandchildren from witches and reptiles, and has given to us his rain. We return thanks to the sun, that he has looked upon the earth with a beneficent eye. Lastly, we return thanks to the Great Spirit, in whom is embodied all goodness, and who directs all things for the good of his children.

(Iroquois, date unknown)

God's Handiwork

*H*ow wonderful, O Lord, are the works of Your hands! The heavens declare Your glory, the arch of sky displays Your handiwork.

The heavens declare the glory of God.

In Your love You have given us the power to behold the beauty of Your world, robed in all its splendor. The sun and the stars, the valleys and hills, the rivers and lakes—all disclose Your presence.

The earth reveals God's eternal presence.

The roaring breakers of the sea tell of Your awesome might; the beasts of the field and the birds of the air bespeak Your wondrous will.

Life comes forth by God's creative will.

In Your goodness You have made us able to hear the music of the world. The raging of the winds, the whisperings of trees in the wood, and the precious voices of loved ones reveal to us that You are in our midst.

A divine voice sings through all creation.

(*Jewish, modern*)

Homage to the Breath of Life

*H*omage to you, Breath of Life, for the whole universe obeys you. You are the ruler of all things on earth, and the foundation of the earth itself.

*H*omage to you, Breath of Life, in the crashes of thunder and in the flashes of lightning. The rain you send gives food to the plants and drink to the animals.

*H*omage to you, Breath of Life, in the changing seasons, in the hot dry sunshine and the cold rain. There is comfort and beauty in every kind of weather.

*T*he plants themselves rejoice in your bounty, praising you in the sweet smell of their blossom. The cattle rejoice, praising you in the pure white milk they give.

*H*omage to you, Breath of Life, in our breathing out and breathing in. At every moment, whatever we are doing, we owe you praise and thanksgiving.

*H*omage to you, Breath of Life, in our birth and in our death. In the whole cycle of life you sustain and inspire us.

*H*omage to you, Breath of Life, in the love and friendship we enjoy. When we love one another, we reflect your infinite love.

*M*en and women rejoice in your bounty, praising you in poem and song. The little children rejoice, praising you in their innocent shrieks of laughter.

(*Atharva-Veda*, c. 1500 B.C.)

Father, We Thank Thee

For flowers that bloom about our feet,
Father, we thank Thee,
For tender grass so fresh and sweet,
Father, we thank Thee,
For the song of bird and hum of bee,
For all things fair we hear or see,
Father in heaven, we thank Thee.

For blue of stream and blue of sky,
Father, we thank Thee,
For pleasant shade of branches high,
Father, we thank Thee,
For fragrant air and cooling breeze,
For beauty of the blooming trees,
Father in heaven, we thank Thee.

For this new morning with its light,
Father, we thank Thee,
For rest and shelter of the night,
Father, we thank Thee,
For health and food, for love and friends,
For everything Thy goodness sends,
Father in heaven, we thank Thee.

(Ralph Waldo Emerson, 1803–82)

Lord, We Thank You

For cities and towns, factories and farms, flowers and trees, sea and sky—

Lord, we praise You for the world and its beauty.

For family and friends, neighbors and cousins—

Lord, we thank You for friendship and love.

For kind hearts, smiling faces, and helping hands—

Lord, we praise You for those who care for others.

For commandments that teach us how to live—

Lord, we thank You for those who help us to understand Your laws.

And for making us one family on earth, the children of One God—

Lord, we praise You, who made all people different, yet alike.

(Jewish, modern)

Invocation of Dsilyi Neyani

Reared with the Mountains!
Lord of the Mountains!
Young Man! Chieftain!
I have made your sacrifice.
I have prepared a smoke for you.
My feet restore thou for me.
My legs restore thou for me.
My body restore thou for me.
My voice thou restore for me.
Restore all for me in beauty.
Make beautiful all that is before me.
Make beautiful all that is behind me.
It is done in beauty.
It is done in beauty.
It is done in beauty.
It is done in beauty.

(Navajo Night Chant, date unknown)

The Flute of the Infinite

The flute of the Infinite is played without ceasing, and its sound is love:
When love renounces all limits, it reaches truth.
How widely the fragrance spreads! It has no end, nothings stands in its
　　way.
The form of this melody is bright like a million suns: incomparably sounds
　　the vina, the vina of the notes of truth.

(Kabir, 1450?–1518)

Planet Earth's Lamentation

Holy of Holies we cry
from Planet Earth—
A tiny speck
in our Universe.
Hear our hearts raised together—
all nations with one voice:
Holy, Holy, Holy!

Lift up our hearts to yours—
close our ranks in brotherhood.
Draw us up to the Galaxies—
lift our minds, souls, all:
Holy, Holy, Holy!

we yearn for your Mighty Presence—
let it all come about.
Purify us for the happening—
make us special among your stars:
Holy, Holy, Holy!

(Regina C. Wilkinson, modern)

The Light of Thy Music

I know not how thou singest, my master! I ever listen in silent amazement.

The light of thy music illumines the world. The life breath of thy music runs from sky to sky. The holy stream of thy music breaks through all stony obstacles and rushes on.

My heart longs to join in thy song, but vainly struggles for a voice. I would speak, but speech breaks not into song, and I cry out baffled. Ah, thou hast made my heart captive in the endless meshes of thy music, my master!

(Rabindranath Tagore, 1861–1941)

Whose Name Is Great

O God, the Father of our Saviour Jesus Christ, Whose name is great, Whose nature is blissful, Whose goodness is inexhaustible, God and Ruler of all things, Who art blessed forever; before Whom stand thousands and thousands, and ten thousand times ten thousand, the hosts of holy angels and archangels; sanctify, O Lord, our souls and bodies and spirits, search our consciences, and cast out of us every evil thought, every base desire, all envy and pride, all wrath and anger, and all that is contrary to Thy holy will. And grant us, O Lord, Lover of men, with a pure heart and contrite soul, to call upon Thee, our holy God and Father Who art in heaven—Amen.

(Liturgy of St. James, second century)

Invocation—Life and Light

O Thou Father of lights, in Thee we live and move and have our being. Thou art our Home; our dwelling is the secret place of the Most High; we abide under the shadow of the Almighty; our refuge is Jehovah. We praise Thee that no evil shall befall those who truly trust Thee, nor shall they be afraid; for Thou hast set Thy love upon them, and they have known Thy name. O Thou Sovereign of Life, Thou art the fountain of life, Thy universe is flooded with life, all space is full of life, for Thou who fillest all things art Thyself life, as Thou are Light and Love. We drink of Thine infinite fulness and, behold, we *live*; and that Life is our Light forevermore.

(A. P. Adams, date unknown)

Anaphora in Honor of Mary

Mary,
you are the extension of heaven
and the foundation of the earth,
the depths of the seas
and the light of the sun,
the beauty of the moon
and the splendor of the stars in the sky.
You are greater than the cherubim,
more eminent than the seraphim,
and more glorious than the chariot of fire.
Your womb bore God, whose majesty overwhelms human beings.
Your lap held the glowing coal.
Your knees propped up the lion of august majesty.
Your hands touched the untouchable
and the fire of the Divinity that lies therein.
Your fingers are like the incandescent tongs
with which the Prophet received the coal of the heavenly oblation.
You are the basket of this bread of burning flame
and the chalice of this wine.

O Mary,
you produce in your womb the fruit of the offering.
We your servants of this sanctuary
ask you to guard us
from the enemy that attacks us,
so that the water and wine are not separated in their mixture,
we too will not be separated from you
and your Son, the Lamb of salvation.

(Ethiopic Anaphora, date unknown)

I Will Give Thanks

O my God, the soul which thou gavest me is pure; thou didst create it, thou didst form it, thou didst breathe it into me; thou preservest it within me; and thou wilt take it from me, but wilt restore it unto me hereafter. So long as the soul is within me, I will give thanks unto thee, O Lord my God and God of my fathers, Sovereign of all worlds, Lord of all souls!

(Hebrew Liturgy)

My Hope and My Heart's Joy

O God, Thou art Life, Wisdom, Truth, Bounty, and Blessedness, the Eternal, the only true Good! My God and my Lord, Thou art my hope and my heart's joy. I confess, with thanksgiving, that Thou hast made me in Thine image, that I may direct all my thoughts to Thee, and love Thee. Lord, make me to know Thee aright, that I may more and more love, and enjoy, and possess Thee. And since, in the life here below, I cannot fully attain this blessedness, let it at least grow in me day by day, until it all be fulfilled at last in the life to come. Here be the knowledge of Thee increased, and there let it be perfected. Here let my love to Thee grow, and there let it ripen; that my joy being here great in hope, may there in fruition be made perfect.

(St. Anselm, 1033–1109)

A Thankful Heart

Lord, Thou hast given me a cell
    Wherein to dwell,
A little house whose humble roof
    Is weatherproof. . . .
Low is my porch as is my fate,
    Both void of state,
And yet the threshold of my door
    Is worn by the poor
Who hither come and freely get
    Good words or meat.
'Tis Thou that crown'st my glittering hearth
    With guileless mirth.
All these and better Thou dost send
    Me to this end,
That I should render for my part
    A thankful heart.

(Robert Herrick, 1591–1674)

No Other Glory

O my God, Thou knowest I have never desired but to love Thee alone. I seek no other glory. Thy Love has gone before me from my childhood, it has grown with my growth, and now it is an abyss the depths of which I cannot fathom.

(St. Therese of Lisieux, 1873—97)

God Dwells in All

The center-fire heaves underneath the earth,
And the earth changes like a human face.
    Thus God dwells in all,
From life's minute beginnings, up at last
To man, the consummation of this scheme
Of being, the completion of this sphere
Of life.

(Robert Browning, 1812–89)

Hearken to My Constant Prayer

O God, do thou thine ear incline,
Protect my children and my kine,
E'en if thou'rt weary, still forbear,
And hearken to my constant prayer.
When shrouded 'neath the cloak of night,
Thy splendors sleep beyond our sight,
And when across the sky by day,
Thou movest, still to thee I pray.
Dread shades of our departed sires,
Ye who can make or mar desires,
Slain by no mortal hand ye dwell,
Beneath the earth, O guard us well.

(Nandi, Kenya, date unknown)

Paradisi Gloria

There is a city, builded by no hand,
    And unapproachable by sea or shore,
And unassailable by any band
    Of storming soldiery for evermore.

In that pure city of the Living Lamb,
    No ray shall fall from satellite or sun,
Or any star; but He who said "I Am"
    Shall be the Light, He and His Holy One.

There we no longer shall divide our time
    By acts of pleasures,—doing petty things
Of work or welfare, merchandise or rhyme;
    But we shall sit beside the silver springs.

That flow from God's own footstool, and behold
    Sages and martyrs, and those blessed few
Who loved us once and were beloved of old,
    To dwell with them and walk with them anew,

In alternations of sublime repose,
    Musical motion, the perpetual play
Of every faculty that Heaven bestows
    Through the bright, busy, and eternal day.

(Author and date unknown)

In the House of Happiness

In the house of long life there I wander,
In the house of happiness there I wander.
Beauty before me, with it I wander.
Beauty behind me, with it I wander.
Beauty below me, with it I wander.
Beauty above me, with it I wander.
Beauty all around me, with it I wander.
In old age traveling, with it I wander.
On the beautiful trail I am, with it I wander.

(Navajo, date unknown)

Invitation to Be Joyful

Let there be joy!
Be truly joyful
here in the place of flowers,
O lord Tecayehuatzi, you
that are adorned with collars.

(Tlapalteuccitzin, a Nahuatl sage, date unknown)

Fragrant Spiritual Flowers

*H*appy is he who opens his heart to you, good Jesus, for you enter and rest there. You bring the midday of heavenly light to the troubled breast, calming every emotion of the heart with the rays of divine peace. You make a bed within the soul with fragrant spiritual flowers, and you lie upon it, so that the soul is filled with the knowledge of you and the joy of your sweetness.

(Aelred of Rievaulx, c.1110–67)

Sunny Days

Lord, with what courage and delight
    I do each thing
When thy least breath sustains my wing!
    I shine and move
    Like those above,
    And (with much gladness
    Quitting sadness)
Make me fair days of every night.

Affliction thus, mere pleasure is,
    And hap what will,
If thou be in't, 'tis welcome still;
    But since thy rays
    In sunny days
    Thou dost thus lend
    And freely spend,
Ah! What shall I return for this?

O that I were all Soul! That thou
    Wouldst make each part
Of this poor, sinful frame pure heart!
    Then would I drown
    My single one
    And to thy praise
    A consort raise
Of Hallelujahs here below.

(Henry Vaughan, 1622–95)

Acknowledgments and Permissions

Bibliography

A Book of Offices and Prayers for Priest and People. New York: Edwin S. Gorham, 1899.

Allen, Paula Gunn. *The Sacred Hoop.* Boston: Beacon Press, 1986.

Appleton, George, ed. *The Oxford Book of Prayer.* Oxford: Oxford University Press, 1985.

Astrov, Margot, ed. *The Winged Serpent.* Boston: Beacon Press, 1992. First published 1946.

Bierhorst, John, ed. *In the Trail of the Wind: American Indian Poems and Ritual Orations.* New York: Farrar, Straus and Giroux, 1971.

Brown, Vinson. *Voices of Earth and Sky.* Harrisburg, Penn.: Stackpole Books, 1974.

Buono, Anthony M. *Favorite Prayers to Our Lady.* New York: Catholic Book Publishing Co., 1991.

Carr, Edwin Hamlin. *"Let Us Give Thanks."* New York: Fleming H. Revell Co., 1929.

Clark, Thomas Curtin, comp. *The Golden Book of Religious Verse.* Garden City, N.Y.: Garden City Publishing Co., 1941.

Coates, Henry T., comp. and ed. *The Fireside Encyclopedia of Poetry.* Philadelphia: Porter & Coates, 1878.

Cronyn, George W. *American Indian Poetry.* New York: Fawcett Columbine, 1962, 1991.

Cruz, Joan Carroll, comp. *Prayers and Heavenly Promises.* Rockford, Ill.: TAN Books and Publishers, 1990.

Davie, Donald. *The New Oxford Book of Christian Verse.* Oxford: Oxford University Press, 1988.

Everett, Joann Marie. *Angel Wisdom and a Woman's Song*. Bucks County, Penn.: Jasmine Press, 1996.

Fisher, A. S. T., comp. *An Anthology of Prayers*. London: Longmans, Green & Co., 1934.

Ford, Rev. James. *A Century of Christian Prayers on Faith, Hope and Charity; with a Morning and Evening Devotion*. 2nd ed. Ipswich, England: John Raw, 1824.

Fox, Selina Fitzherbert, comp. *A Chain of Prayer Across the Ages: Forty Centuries of Prayer, 2000 B.C.–A.D. 1941*. London: John Murray, 1913, 1941.

Gates of Prayer. New York: Central Conference of American Rabbis, 1975.

Hart, Rev. Samuel, comp. *A Manual of Short Daily Prayers for Families*. New York: Longmans, Green & Co., 1902.

Hobe, Phyllis. *The Guideposts Handbook of Prayer*. Carmel, N.Y.: Guideposts, 1982.

Kempis, Thomas à. *The Imitation of Christ*. Rockford, Ill.: TAN Books and Publishers, 1989.

Knowles, Canon. *Not Changed But Glorified*. New York: James Pott & Co., 1896.

Leon-Portilla, Miguel, ed. *Native Mesoamerican Spirituality*. New York: Paulist Press, 1980.

MacCrocaigh, R., transl. *Prayers of the Gael*. London: Sands & Co., 1914.

Martin, Hugh, ed. *A Book of Prayers for Schools*. London: Student Christian Movement Press, 1936.

Meyer, Lucy Rider. *Some Little Prayers*. Cincinnati: Jennings and Graham, 1907.

Millgian, Harold Vincent, ed. *The Best Loved Hymns and Prayers of the American People*. Garden City, N.Y.: Halcyon House, 1942.

Morrow, Abbie C. *Prayers for Public Worship, Private Devotion, Personal Ministry*. New York: M. E. Munson, 1902.

Noyes, Morgan Phelps. *Prayers for Services*. New York: Charles Scribner's Sons, 1934.

Okada, Mochiki. *Johrei: Divine Light of Salvation*. Kyoto, Japan: The Society of Johrei, 1984.

Page, Herman, and Laidlaw, Gilbert, adapters and compilers. *Prayers*. New York: Edwin S. Gorham, 1918.

Pauli, Max. *Prayers for the Time Being*. Ligouri, Mo.: Ligouri Publications, 1974.

Prayers Ancient and Modern. New York: Doubleday & McClure Co., 1897.

Ryan, Marah Ellis, comp. *Pagan Prayers*. Chicago: A. C. McClurg & Co., 1913.

Shorter, Aylward. *Prayer in the Religious Traditions of Africa*. London: Oxford University Press, 1975.

Stewart, Elinor Cochrane. *Prayers of Hope and Gladness*. New York: Pevensey Press, 1930.

Tagore, Rabindranath. *Gitanjali*. New York: The Macmillan Co., 1916.

Tagore, Rabindranath, transl. *Songs of Kabir*. New York: The Macmillan Co., 1915.

The New Guideposts Treasury of Prayer. Carmel, N.Y.: Guideposts, 1991.

The Voices of the Saints. Selected and arranged by Francis W. Johnston. Rockford, Ill.: TAN Books and Publishers, 1965.

Thirkield, Wilbur Patterson, ed. and comp. *Service and Prayers for Church and Home*. New York: The Methodist Book Concern, 1918.

Tileston, Mary W., comp. *Great Souls at Prayer*. London: H. R. Allenson Ltd., 1898.

Thoughts of St. Therese. Rockford, Ill.: TAN Books and Publishers, 1988. First published 1915.

Van de Weyer, Robert, comp. *The HarperCollins Book of Prayers*. San Francisco: HarperSanFrancisco, 1993.

Wilkinson, Rosemary Regina Challoner. *Poetry: Nature*. San Francisco: EJ Co., 1996.

Williams, Monier. *Religious Thought and Life in India.* New Delhi: Oriental Books Reprint Corp., 1974. First published 1883.

Wood, L. S. *A Book of English Verse on Infancy and Childhood.* London: Macmillan and Co. Ltd., 1921.

Woolley, Reginald Maxwell, transl. *Coptic Offices.* New York: The Macmillan Co., 1930.

Yogananda, Paramahansa. *Songs of the Soul.* Los Angeles: Self-Realization Fellowship, 1983.

LIGHTNER PHOTOGRAPHY, INC.

ROSEMARY ELLEN GUILEY is a renowned expert on spirituality, mystical and exceptional human experience, and the paranormal. She is a frequent and popular lecturer on such topics as angels, prayer, healing, dreams, alchemy, spiritual awakenings, and mysteries of the unknown. She serves on the board of trustees for the Academy of Religion and Psychical Research. Among her previous books are *Blessings: Prayers for the Home and Family*, *The Miracle of Prayer*, *Angels of Mercy*, and *Tales of Reincarnation*, all published by Pocket Books. She lives with her husband near Annapolis, Maryland.